LOVE Y♥U BIG

The Heart Journey of Adoption

KATHLEEN KJOLHAUG

Published by
SugarBrooke Creative Services
McIntosh, Minnesota 56556
www.sugarbrookecreative.com
(701) 361-1368

Design by Katie Krogstad

Scripture taken from the New King James Version. Copyright © 1982 by Thomas Nelson, Inc. Used by permission. All rights reserved.

Scripture taken from the HOLY BIBLE, NEW INTERNATIONAL VERSION®. Copyright © 1973, 1978, 1984 Biblica.
Used by permission of Zondervan. All rights reserved.

Scripture texts in this work are taken from the *New American Bible with Revised New Testament and Revised Psalms* © 1991, 1986, 1970 Confraternity of Christian Doctrine, Washington, D.C. and are used by permission of the copyright owner. All Rights Reserved.
No part of the *New American Bible* may be reproduced in any form without permission in writing from the copyright owner.

Copyright © 2010 by Kathleen Kjolhaug. All Rights Reserved.
No part of this book may be reproduced without prior written permission of the publisher or author. Reviewers may quote passages in articles & reviews.

ISBN-13: 978-0-9826515-0-6

Printed in the United States of America

This book is lovingly dedicated to:

Rebekah Alice

&

Esther Joy

You have opened up our hearts to places we never knew existed. God bless the journey He has for you. We are honored to be a part of it.

*Love,
Mom & Dad
Luke, Maria, Heidi, & Christopher*

TABLE OF CONTENTS

Foreword by Luke Kjolhaug	6
Introduction	9
Lady...Hey Lady	11
Far Away Places	17
The Journey Begins	23
The Plans I have for You	33
The Airport	59
The Journey Home	65
The Days & Weeks Ahead	69
The Golden Ticket	77
Ducky Doolittle	81
Miracle on 440th Street	85

FOREWORD

People, in general, are not complicated. We all have basic instincts, needs, and desires. Yet so often the simple actions which would fill the holes, hurts, and gaps in the lives of others are not taken. Above all, it seems to me that we have the need to love, and to be loved by the lives around us. There is no action which, driven by pure loving-kindness and selflessness, will return void. It is true we don't always get to sow the seeds, or even see the reaping, but that seed has nonetheless been planted in another human being made in the very image of God. That is not something to be taken lightly or ignored.

When we openly pour ourselves—our gifts, talents, dreams, words, time, money—out to others, we truly are fulfilling the greatest commandment of all. There is a passion and power in such other-centered sacrifice that we can often only stand back in awe as we watch our Creator do His work. It is a reward in and of itself, and making a meaningful difference in the life of another draws us even closer to our image-bearer, the center from which all love emanates.

What a gift, and what an opportunity we have been given. How many times day in and day out do we fail to even recognize the hurts in our brother's life, being so wrapped up in our own concerns. What would happen if we shifted the focus just a little bit? When we choose to love another, the blessings are always reflected back, oftentimes with an amplified intensity. We begin to give, begin to make that painful first step of self-sacrifice, and, little by little, we begin to realize that the source of that love is continually pouring out—actually brimming over. There is an endless supply to give, and it is not coming from us. How deep and how mighty that well-spring can be once we decide to step in and let it wash over.

    We will always be imperfect people with only an imperfect love to give, but that itself can be an encouragement when viewed through the eyes of a fellow sufferer. If we can make the decision to "love as He first loved us," whatever that may mean to each person in this vast and varied sea of lives, the result will be greater than anything we can imagine. He gives us life, passion, and drive for a reason, and only by reaching out and touching the lives of others can we truthfully know the real power of love. We are never alone, and it always helps to be reminded of that.

Luke Kjolhaug
(Oldest brother of Rebekah & Esther)

Is there room at the Inn?
Room for one...just one more?

Introduction

This book was birthed from a heart to share our personal story of adoption. Hopefully, by taking the journey along with us, it will help you understand the road traveled. Although each person's adoption experience is so very different, the common thread that unites…is the heart. That will forever remain constant. To those who are thinking about the process of adoption, may this book help you to know that it is not only possible but that it can be incredibly fulfilling. To those who will never go through the process, may you better understand the lives of others who do. May you see it as a connecting gift spanning the globe. The stories are true. The lives that will forever be changed are real. My prayer for each reader is that your lives, too, will forever be changed through the unfailing promises of His word and the words written upon the pages that follow.

Kathleen

Kathleen Kjolhaug

Lady...Hey Lady!

Our youngest chirped, swatted, and waved for attention from the tall, stiff figured woman standing before her. Once again, I heard her hardy little voice demanding, this time in a tone a tad more adamant, "Lady! Hey lady!" She spoke directly facing her opponent with her hands on hips.

Standing beside this five year old daughter of ours was her seven year old sister, floundering with a facial expression that longed to make sense of what she was observing. She knew not what to do, nor did she attempt to make a move in either direction of the two parties facing off.

Turning from my conversation with the owner of the clothing store in which we stood, I looked to see what the ruckus was all about. It took mere seconds to realize the dilemma. One of our newly adopted daughters, having arrived just a few weeks prior from Chennai, India, was visibly frustrated with the lack of response from her one way conversation. She continued to jump, jiggle, and wiggle for attention as she apparently was not used to being ignored by those with whom she chose to converse.

Clearly she had not been in the United States long enough to realize proper etiquette in this situation. Presenting itself anew to her was not only a perfect stranger, but the stranger she stood toe to toe with was none-other than the store mannequin!

Gathering my thoughts, while trying not to give off an *air* of total dismay, I searched for words she might understand. "Esther..." I chided, "...that's not a lady. That's a big dolly!" I pulled her nearer to her object of frustration and had her stroke the firm, plastic arms. To her surprise, it really was just a big *dolly*. With a burst of giggles, she and her sister caught on to the unfolding reality as well as to the humor at hand.

Their beginning days within our household brought opportunities to build foundations, and soon, their lives began to make sense in a world that was strangely unfamiliar.

But...the heart journey to adopt began long ago...

"Before I formed you in the womb, I knew you."
Jeremiah 1:5

Marriage brought with it, life on the family homestead. It was a privilege to carry on the tradition of making this century farm our home.

One by one, we filled the second story bedrooms. There were four rooms; we had four children. Although our first born didn't arrive until our early thirties, by the time we'd hit thirty-five, we had four children, ages four and under.

We liked the farm, but yet longed to make an impact beyond its borders. Simply put, there was a seed planted in my heart as a child. The desire sprouting from that seed always included working with others around the world, and that desire would not leave.

Promises to serve overseas were made, but with each passing year, the time just never seemed right. When two years slipped by, it appeared that five would be a more appropriate time frame. When five years arrived, we were knee deep in children…and elbow deep in diapers.

As time passed, I wrote down our desires, our dreams, our longings. I penned a future of hope and trust in what was not yet seen. Like the birth of our Savior so many years ago, we waited. When all was yet a silent night, we waited. It was not easy to see how the early promises within our marriage would be fulfilled, but there was a plan unfolding… as we waited…still.

And…while we waited, we unknowingly prepared our hearts. *"Little friends in jungle deep…like to rock themselves to sleep."* Many evenings we would find our four little ones piled within our arms as these words were read from one of their favorite childhood storybooks. In hopes that they might see a bigger world…we read.

When the reading stopped, and all were tucked in, my writing would begin. The dreams to collect those who were not yet in our arms was, by hindsight, always just under the surface of my heart. It was illustrated in the recounting of an evening walk taken down our country road…all the while…dreaming.

FAR AWAY PLACES

Oh...for the escape...the freedom...the journeys to foreign places far and near. I run to...I run from...I am not sure from what, or to whom I run, but I run. I run briskly and take in the fresh freedoms from the vastness of the blowing breezes.

These breezes feel like Paraguay. The quiet, desolate, yet peaceful tranquility in the campo (countryside) between the farm houses awakens my interest to see what lies ahead. The faint smell of home fires burning is in the air, while the warmth from them dries the clothes which were freshly hand-washed today. These fires warm the chipa (cheese bread) and sopa (soup) for the neighborly drop-ins to share. The terere (tea drink) is slowly passed from brother to brother...sister to sister. Oh, my Paraguay.

Moving on brings the openness of the pampas (grasslands) gathering in its Argentina. I can faintly see the silhouettes of three caballeros (cowboys) ahead. The pulsating, soothing hoof beats from their horses help the dust to rise upwards in billows of gray fog. Their animals do not pause, but carry them on to the mission ahead. Easy does it...and on they pass. Oh, my Argentina.

Overhead are the stars, decorating the darkness in an igloo shaped dome that covers the land securely for all to be comfortably enclosed. Oh…the reflective colors cascading from the northern lights of Alaska. I see the snow white covered tundra pitted beside me, just feet away from where my own are walking…walking on as briskly as the evening air is being taken in. Briefly, I pause in the still quiet night to enjoy the landscape of the stars blanketing my mood. They twinkle, and for a moment, I can feel their warmth emitted to all below. Oh, my Alaska.

Ahead lie the horizons of Africa. Oh…the sunsets you offer. They radiate tones of rich reds, oranges, and yellows melting to where the rubber meets the road. It's as if a huge umbrella opened up enclosing the day to any who dare take note of this branding event. The markings of a day's end softly invites, yet boldly states that whether one had to strive or merely stride through the day, in the end, we remain as brothers. All will be well until tomorrow. As for the few fallen twigs gathered and lit for warmth…we give thanks. Oh, my Africa.

I slip back from where I've come in order to get where I must go. I must go home. For the night is calling me home. I must leave, but only for now. For tomorrow, I may pass by and dream once more of longings and yearnings. The sights, sounds, and scents of being part of a bigger world has been expanding my heart, and on I run…down the gravel path and back onto the weathered wooden porch of our country home. The front door breathes life in, it welcomes as it opens, and the burst of warmth pours out into the coolness of the evening where I stand. This sanctuary allows me to dream and renew this strength that calls…to be still and know that You are God.

"For I tell you that out of these stones God can raise up children for Abraham."
Luke 3:8

Fifteen years into our marriage we decided the time was right to do an outreach trip overseas. We'd been receiving e-mails from a children's home in Costa Rica. It was a puzzle as to how we ended up on their mailing list, but answering the nudge, my husband and I agreed to tap open a few doors.

The calling took the form of volunteering at the "Homes of Life" in Atenas, Costa Rica. We were introduced to dozens of abandoned and abused children living on this mission compound. Each day drew us in like bees to honey. We savored every miraculous minute with Tim and Dena, the directors, who poured into the lives of children. When the ten day trip was completed, the imprint upon our hearts could not have been deeper.

We'd barely arrived home when our four children began pleading with us to bring home the little brother/sister team we'd fallen in love with. At the "Homes of Life," we'd held, played with, and comforted many children. But without fail, when I glanced over at any of my own, they'd be fussing over at least one of the two in the sibling pair.

They continued to raise their voices on behalf of the two needing a family. As affirmation would have it, we received an e-mail informing us that these two little ones were going to be up for adoption.

One phone call to my husband brought forth words that cinched the heart strings. "Do what you need to do to begin the process!" And…we did.

THE JOURNEY BEGINS...

"The man with two tunics should share with him who has none, and the one who has food should do the same."
Luke 3:11

From the beginning, there was inner turmoil instead of a peace that passes all understanding. And...the journal entries said it all.

> 4-14-99 *"I awoke this morning from sleep that was much needed. That pit...that pit in your stomach when something the evening before has taken place...is sitting center. The adoption process began 3 months ago. From the beginning, our hearts have been sunk into the hearts of these 2 children. We've been making plans to expand our home in order to be ready for their arrival. I have envisioned them coming to school with me, running across our lawn, and being taught in love from their brothers and sisters. We have been in prayer, to the best of our ability, trying

to turn it over to Him. We have been praying, 'Your will,' and have been asking that if He has a better plan, to make it known. We want only His best. Our adoption agency, Love Basket, has been most encouraging. However, apparently our correspondence with Costa Rica has not been as strong. In that I am feeling anxiety instead of peace. Something more is going on. I sent an e-mail, but no response has come."

We carried on as best we could with our household routines. Talking about this throughout the day came naturally. Paper work, phone calls, and the schedules that kept us on track were a part of those conversations. However, knowing that things were not in our control brought challenges. And, on the top of that list, was the issue of trust.

"Make each day a prayer. Offer up everything you do… for Him!" Those were mom's words. She believed them, and she lived by them. Mom's been gone for many years now, but I've clung to those words. Each breath, each moment, each day as we walked through this process, we could do nothing but trust that whatever lie ahead would be His best. And in order to know what that best was, we simply needed to place one foot in front of the other in order to see where the path would lead.

> *"Now to Him who is able to do immeasurably beyond all we ask or imagine, be all glory forever and ever."*
> **Ephesians 3:20-21**

And the journal entries continued…

> 4-15-99 "We pray for you, little ones. We prayed that you grow strong in the Lord…that you smile… His smile…that you reach out, touch and feel His firm hands guiding and holding you. To not see the path ahead…or the big picture…'tis hard to trust. I must. We must. We know you are wiser, Lord. I sometimes find a little peace in the midst of the disturbances."

The journal entries ranged from fear, to hope, and back again. The cycle of ups and downs came weekly…if not daily and truth-be-told…sometimes hourly. Having never traveled down this road before, it felt more like walking on cobblestones than pavement. A little pit here, another stone to turn there, made this bumpy path our home for the next several months and one from which we would never want to depart.

4-17-99 *"Today I received an e-mail from Costa Rica. They said you were well. They haven't spoken to your social worker yet, and do not know the status of your case. She'll let us know more soon. Good night my children...may His angels watch over you both and all of your precious friends."*

7-15-99 *"I spoke with Love Basket today. They told us our attorney's name in Costa Rica. His wife speaks English. Our home study will be done soon. It was encouraging to get any kind of information! So many people are praying for you."*

However, just below that journal entry was a quote inscribed upon the page:

*** Philippians 4:6. *"Be anxious for nothing, but in everything by prayer and supplication, with thanksgiving, let your requests be made known to God."*

The triple star beside it was proof enough that I was trying to convince myself that things would be OK. This verse brought no promise that anything would turn out as planned. It was simply a message that we were to rail on heaven's doors and trust that what would take place…would be heaven sent.

> *"Present your needs to God in prayer and petitions full of gratitude. Then God's own peace, which is beyond all understanding, will stand guard over your hearts and minds in Christ Jesus."*
> **Philippians 4:6-9**

7-21-99 *"I called Love Basket. They said our fingerprints cleared on June 23, and all looks good so far. Another little ray of hope. We sure wish you were here. God's blessings on you little ones. You are His! Love, Mom"*

7-30-99 *"Our agency received the papers back from the Consulate in Costa Rica. Now, our agency needs to pass them on to Tim and Dena so they may be translated. We continue adding onto our home so all will be settled before you get here. I miss you!"*

Within four days, the journal entries took a dramatic turn

down a road we had no choice but to travel. This first entry appeared to be more of a desperate bargaining tool with God.

> *8-4-99 1 Samuel 1:11 "If you will...remember me, and not forget your servant but give her a son, then I will give him to the Lord for all the days of his life."*

It was nine days later we received the knee buckling news.

> *8-13-99 "It's been strangely quiet. I have requested prayer by many. Last night we received an e-mail from Costa Rica which said that you may be going to a couple in Italy! We cried. Yet, we feel a strange peace and picture you among that warm culture being loved up by another family. The Italian language is so similar to Spanish. You will feel at home there. I am grieving. I stare at the lily white dress I bought for you, my daughter. I look in vain for the little girl to breathe life into it. We bought a little bug light up shirt for you too, my son. We will send it. Not yet though. First, we will pray. **Help us Dear Lord!**"*

"Be still and know that I am God."
Psalm 46:10

8-18-99 "It's still so quiet. As far as we know, your lives are directed towards Italy. That is a good place for you. It's just that we wanted to be the ones to love you, to hold you, and to laugh with you. We wanted to be the ones to teach you that the world is kind. We continue to pray; we continue to prepare. I am still feeling like I should have been more in tune…to perhaps have had the paperwork in along with our names, so the court system could have known that the process was nearing completion on our end. We were cautioned to wait. We waited. Now, it looks like we will wait on His will alone. Amen."

8-20-99 "Why? Why were our hearts opened? Why were we being prepared? Why? Did I not listen? I feel like I didn't. Was I not in tune with Your direction, Lord? Was the best for them elsewhere? Was all of this meant to be? I sensed you guiding *me like a bumper car. Did I not jump in and drive when you needed a driver? Was I taking this all too cautiously? Should I have run more with abandoned for the abandoned? Did I not ask the right questions? Need I learn more trust? WHY? We have hope. The gospel tells us that. It's so quiet. Yet, the doors still appear to be falling gently open. It's so quiet... quiet... so quiet!"*

And, I thank God for the gift of writing. Words from journal entries convey details, but it went deep...so much deeper. The following story was birthed from this pain.

The Plans I Have for You

"Pete! Come here…quick!" I yelled at the top of my voice from a nearby room, my desperate heart pounding. The computer monitor flashed before us conveying an urgent message. The reality of what it meant began to sink in, and tears quickly reached the surface of my eyes. My legs felt like pools of melting rubber, hanging limp beneath my chair as I stared at the words upon the screen.

Pete stood quietly beside me, motionless, except for the moving of his arm which now rested upon my shoulder.

"How do we tell the kids?" I cried, tears now spilling down my cheeks. Silent prayers were raised in unison as each tear fell.

"I don't know," he simply responded in heavy tones that matched the unseen weight bearing down on his heart.

It had been an emotional investment to say the least. Our family had begun the adoption process for two children we'd recently met overseas. The pair needed placement more quickly than planned. Now, their new home was ready for them. Their new home was ready alright, but it was across the ocean from where they presently lived, and across the ocean from us! They were going to Italy!

Breaking the news to our children brought forth statements of disbelief. They questioned the possibility that a mistake was made. And…if that were the case, they'd be coming after all!

"No," I reassured each one. "Our paperwork was not yet complete, and although we'd prayed for these children as our own, clearly the Lord had other plans." The words tumbled smoothly from my mouth, echoing a strength that was nowhere to be found.

The next few days brought heaviness within our home… like a fog that would not lift. As we continued communication with our adoption agency, the best we could do was to verbalize hope, feel the disappointment, and wait.

The words from Jeremiah 29:11 brought comfort. *"For I know the plans I have for you,"* declares the Lord, *"plans to prosper you and not to harm you, plans to give you a hope and a future."*

Knowing that He would not only bring comfort to us, but to our two precious children whom we thought would be ours, brought little relief at the moment. The two little children we longed for were going to another home in order to give them a future and a hope…and the only thing we knew was that we must continue to trust.

"You are to distribute this land among yourselves

according to the tribes of Israel. You are to allot it as an inheritance for yourselves and for the aliens who have settled among you and who have children. You are to consider them as native-born Israelites; along with you they are to be allotted an inheritance among the tribes of Israel. In whatever tribe the alien settles, there you are to give him his inheritance; declares the sovereign Lord." **Ezekiel 47:21-22**

Several times along the journey, this verse was the only thing we could cling to. It was first entered into my journal in May, 1999 - and laid the foundation of hope through February, 2001. It would remain a constant reminder that there was a plan. We clung to those words from Ezekiel like a child with a blanket, and we would not relinquish the hope they brought.

> 8-24-99 "I spoke with Love Basket today. They assured us that the Lord has a plan and that we did nothing to make things happen the way they did. I feel He is preparing our hearts for **His best**. We are healing in hope.
>
> They spoke to us of the need to adopt girls from the country of India. My heart has always held a special place for that country. It reminds me of the

work of Mother Teresa. Through the years, the Lord plants seeds upon our journey in life, and in due season, they grow. He can reap the harvest. I have hope. Lord, You gently open the doors we are tapping. I do not want to push and shove to make it mine...but truly desire what is Thine. The agency assured us that the Lord has something WONDERFUL in store for us, and when we see it, we will be so very blessed!"

> "The promises of the Lord are sure."
> **Psalm 12:7**

These words looked good on paper, but within my heart there was war raging. The conflict was between two opposing forces. The first being the grief imploding from within about the earlier adoption that did not go through...to the opposite end of trying desperately to reach for what was to come...and not being able to grab hold of any hope whatsoever.

Words of anger flowed through my mind, and I longed to speak them aloud. Words like, "What do you know? Just let me feel the hurt! Let me take on the motherly guilt of this!" I wanted to bury myself in the pain, which then soon turned into a lack of trust.

However, our agency chose truth instead of the circumstances on display. Their mission statement was founded on the word of God, and they would not depart from it. In that, we found the strength we needed to carry on. They believed there was a plan, and that in due season, we would see the fruit of what that would look like. In other words, they were asking us to trust.

The next three journal entries were all Bible verses. To these words we held on tightly!

8-25-99 2 Peter 3:9 "The Lord does not delay in keeping His promise...though some consider it delay."

John 1:5 "God is Light and in Him there is no darkness!"

Psalm 91:1-2, 15 "He who dwells in the shelter of the Most High will rest in the shadow of the Almighty. I will say of the Lord, He is my refuge and my fortress, my God in whom I trust. I will deliver him."

> *"Bow humbly under God's mighty hand so that in due time, He may lift you high."*
> **1 Peter 5:6**

Three days later…a break through. Words of hope were written from a trust deep within.

> *8-28-99 "Lord, guide us and prepare both of our hearts for this new little one that <u>is</u> coming."*

Originally preparing for two made the decision to move forward for a single adoption feel sort of odd, but it looked to be the only choice we would have at this time. We moved forward out of obedience. "Lord haste the day when my faith shall be sight…" The old hymn ran its course in the most literal way possible, and our faith was our sight at this point in the crossroads.

> *1 Peter 1:17 "Conduct yourselves reverently during your sojourn in a strange land."*

The entry continues...

"I had a dream last night. I was running in a field, and there were snakes. There was a big one that was not from here. As I ran, I tried to out run it. It came towards me, but then went past me. A little girl went running up the hill. The snake turned, followed, and swallowed. If I were not there to get her out, she would have been swallowed up for good. The dream stopped. It left me with the feeling that what we were going to decide to do was very important in the life of another."

8-29-99 "Our peace is in Him, not our circumstances. It is still so very quiet! Quiet that is, until I read 3 John, "Dear friend, You are faithful in what you are doing for the brothers, even though they are strangers to you.""

9-5-99 Psalm 63:8-9 "My whole being follows hard after You and clings closely to You. Thy right hand holds me."

Isaiah 41:13 "For I am the Lord, your God, who takes hold of your right hand and says to you, 'Do not fear; I will help you.'"

"Surety, safety, songs, security, strength…these are all blessings for us today. If He is holding us, dear one, He is holding you too. Monday we go to Duluth for our home study."

> "Delight yourself in the Lord, and He will
> give you the desires of your heart."
> **Psalm 37:4**

"We open our hearts up to you, little one. We have room at the Inn. In our hearts and in our home, we have room."

9-6-99 "I feel like celebrating your birthday! Today we went for our home study. We feel that perhaps the door to India is opening. We will see. You are already born. You are there…just not here. You are ours. Amen! Your dad and I are talking and just now realizing that we already have a child, and it is a grand feeling! We just don't know one another yet... but the Lord does. He has a plan!! We will wait on Him."

Philippians 4:6-9 "Present your needs to God in every form of prayer and in petitions full of gratitude. Then God's own peace, which is beyond all understanding, will stand guard over your hearts and minds, in Christ Jesus."

Philippians 4:1 "Continue, my dear ones, to stand firm in the Lord."

"We believe, dear one, that you will be coming from the city of Chennai. We await. All is still. All is quiet. We await. Our final home study is to be done this Wednesday. Your brothers and sisters only concern is, 'Will we get her for sure? For sure mom, will we get her?' They tell their friends about you. They are helping to think of a name, which you already have in the heart of the Lord! We await His word. We feel peace. We are tapping the doors open, one step at a time. Somehow, I feel in my heart that Spring will bring you here."

"But Ruth said, 'Do not ask me to abandon or forsake you. For wherever you go, I will go, wherever you lodge, I will lodge, your people shall be my people, and your God shall be my God too.'"
Ruth 1:16

10-2-99 "I had a vision in church today. You ran up from the back of church, down the aisle, arms up and the warmth of picking you up and holding you in His warmth was real. You are His. You are part of the plan of Love through Him. It's His plan! It is to be. You are chosen. I give it to Him clearly and look up...awaiting in expectation for Him to move."

12-25-99 Christmas Day. "Two presents are waiting for you. Your brothers and sisters had you on their Christmas list. Your new little cousin will be arriving from Guatemala in February. It is all in His timing!"

12-28-99 "The paper work continues. We have been living at grandpa and grandma's house for the past *two months. We are back now and able to focus. All in His timing. Emotionally and physically we were exhausted. It's time now...time to move forward."*

The Christmas season ended with the promises from
1 Peter 1:8-12...

"Though you have not seen him, you love him, and even though you do not see him now, you believe in him and are filled with an inexpressible and glorious joy, for you are receiving the goal of your faith, the salvation of your souls. Concerning this salvation, the prophets, who spoke of the grace that was to come to you, searched intently and with the greatest care, trying to find out the time and circumstances to which the Spirit of Christ in them was pointing when he predicted the sufferings of Christ and the glories that would follow... Even the angels long to look into these things."

With a heart for adoption, believing that we too have been adopted by God into his family, one cannot help but know the truth these words reveal.

"I will not leave you orphaned; I will come back to you."
John 14:18

The next journal entry was not written until January.

> **1-24-00** "We await your arrival. We have decided that it is the Lord who is choosing you. He did such a great job bringing us the four we already have, that we know He can choose the fifth! We finished a pile of papers in the second packet and have almost completed packet three as well. We wait. We pray. We had a family meeting this week. We discussed where you'll be sleeping, how everyone will be carrying out their roles in our home in a better way than what they have been doing. Your sisters fear you'll never come. Your brothers want us to full speed ahead with the projected time frame. 'Because,' they insist, 'That's why we added on!' They also think it'll be neat having a new sister to have in the family."

The journal entry continues by expressing more concerns.

> "Sometimes, I wonder if our home will be what's best for you. We have hearts for you. We have room and

love for you. Then, doubt and lack of trust creep in. I grieve that you will not know your own rich culture. I feel sadness for the circumstances that bring you to our home; you will not know your family background fully. I wonder if you will feel resentment at having no voice in the process. Someday… I hope your heart will sing knowing God's hands have provided. You come to us from a loving children's home in India. There have been other brothers and sisters in Christ caring, guiding, and loving you. You have been set apart for a time to grow, love, and be guided in our home. I hope your heart will feel free to search, cry, heal, and grow in the areas needed. We support and love you just as you are. I pray we can be what you need us to be for you."

"Looking unto Jesus, the author and finisher of our faith."
Hebrews 12:2

2-9-00 "They forwarded our home study to New Delhi in case our referral will be from there. We will see…He knows. As I focused on all of the obstacles, I read tonight that sometimes detours cause us to take our eyes off the goal. We may be distracted by looking at obstacles or problems, but we must keep our eyes focused on our goal. He, who is with us at the beginning of the race and will see us through to the end, accompanies us in the middle as well. As I opened a devotional, the words were an encouragement. I draw strength. This journal is nearing an end, and I know this process is nearing an end as well!"

2-20-00 "Sunday's bulletin had a story in it about a family that was older and decided to raise two more children. Pete showed it to me and just smiled!"

3-13-00 "We wait in peaceful expectation. Kate, from Love Basket, is back from India with news of you. I haven't spoken to her yet…we wait to hear. Perhaps Wednesday I will call. We pray for your heart to be prepared and receptive for all He holds for you."

Four days went by before we finally heard from Kate. And...it couldn't have been better if we would have designed the script ourselves!

> 3-17-00 "Kate called today! AND...did she have news! I've been praying for three things. Ultimately, these three things were the desires of my heart...signs if you will...that the referral would be from Him and Him alone.
>
> 1. That we would be able to accept the first referral... not wanting to pick a child based on a photograph.
> 2. That we would get some information about your background as to why you were placed in the children's home.
> 3. I've been praying that you have had opportunity to bond with others so that when you come here, it would be an easy transition for you. He has granted more than my heart's desire! As I relayed the information to Pete...he just beamed and when I told him your names (plural!!) your

birth mother had given you...he said, "I like those! Think of the Bible and what those women stood for!"

> *"I will put my trust in Him; here am I and the children whom God has given me."*
> **Hebrews 2:13**

Yes, the word Pete used was **women**! The miracle that unfolded was that when Love Basket called, they had a sibling pair that needed placement. Two little girls, Rebekah...age 7... and Esther...age 5, needed a home. The timing of it all was no less than a miracle. In the midst of our hearts being broken when the first sibling pair went to Italy, those who were in line to adopt Rebekah and Esther had backed away from the adoption process. These two little girls had been waiting for adoption clearance, and when it finally came, the couple in line to receive them had changed their mind. As our Love Basket family had prayed, they felt that we might consider this little pair. And... of course...we considered it alright. We considered it for approximately thirty seconds flat before we were able to take a breath and process the information about which they spoke.

3-17-00 (continued): "Sometimes, in life, we feel like we are not sure we are on the right path. Then, every so often, we catch a glimpse of the bigger picture, and He blesses us with the knowledge that He truly is at work...working overtime. His plan is so big. Mother Teresa's words echo within me daily, 'We are simply pencils in His hands.' We wait for more information that will be arriving in the mail next week!"

"I will praise Your name forever and ever."
Psalm 145:2

3-22-00 "Today...over the intercom...the school secretary announced, 'Your express mail package is in the Post Office, do you want the mailman to bring it in with the regular mail, or go pick it up now?' I RAN all the way, hugging it as I took it over to Pete's office so we could open it together. He was gone. I called him on the cell phone, and he urged me to open it immediately. Of course...I did! I saw your precious faces for the first time! I must have looked at your picture twenty times. Driving to Pete's office after work, I slipped your pictures out and it was love at first sight! 'Aren't they cute little girls?' We talked about you when he came home, and as he put the file on the counter said, 'Those are the ones!' Initially, we had agreed not to share any information with your brothers and sisters until the time was closer. We were afraid that once again, they might be disappointed if things did not work out. However, Pete couldn't wait! He called to your brothers and sisters and in an instant, you won the hearts of the four onlookers!"

I vividly remember their reaction! As they looked at the picture of you standing together, they asked, 'Which one is ours?' When we told them that you both would be ours…they simply could not believe it and immediately asked your names. They were ecstatic!

4-13-00 "Your dad hung your photos on our fridge. You are his little girls! Grandpa and

Grandma have been showing your pictures to people. Your cousins are asking about you!"

4-15-00 "I'm working today, little ones. Our hearts are being prepared. We wait. You are fearfully and wonderfully made. We wait."

5-11-00 "Our papers are in Chicago now and will be returned to Love Basket soon. They will then be sent to India to start the final legal process there. At times the wait seems so long but all is still peaceful.

I wrote you a letter, but they suggested that we wait until the time gets nearer. We wait. It could be another year...we wait."

5-30-00 "Your brothers bought a few crayons and color books for you. When you arrive, you'll have a few treasures."

"Don't be impatient for the Lord to act. Keep traveling steadily along His pathway and in due season He will honor you with every blessing."
Psalm 37:34

6-11-00 "We received your updated photos. Reports are that when Love Basket visited you, you were pretty shy. You played catch with them, and they watched as you played with other kids. They reported that you were healthy and happy. We wait!"

6-15-00 "We received your video and heard your sweet voices. We saw your awesome smiles and the tender love from others. Pictures are nice as an introduction, but this video helped us to see your facial expressions and a little of your personalities. The nursery rhymes you perform are so fun to watch, and you're counting to ten so well! Your enunciation is so clear and your smiles huge!"

7-25-00 "The message we are getting is 'Be prepared!' Our friends from Costa Rica came to visit. The children did cartwheels in the new addition...

affirmation of the very thing I desired from the bigger space we now have!"

8-11-00 "Love Basket called today and some papers were lost in Delhi. We scrambled, and we sent out duplicate copies the same day!"

8-25-00 "People are asking about you all the time. They wait with us!"

11-18-00 "About three weeks ago, you had your court date in India. It went well. A social worker was assigned to you, and you will have two court hearings coming up soon. I know He will bless our endeavors. Love, Mom."

11-22-00 "We received a phone call today from Love Basket. Your paper work has gone through in India and we are officially your mom and dad. We were granted guardianship. We've been your mom and dad from the start, however, now it is legal! Amen."

"These are the people of the Lord, yet they had to leave their land... Thus says the Lord God: Not for your sakes do I act, house of Israel, but for the sake of my holy name... Thus the nations shall know that I am the Lord."
Ezekiel 36:20-22

1-06-01 "Yesterday, I mailed off the final papers. This should prepare the way for your passports from both countries. Some documents were given to us which included personal information about your lives. We had been wondering what your middle names should be, but now we know. We read, within those documents, that your mother's name was Joy and your grandmother's name was Alice. We now know you are to be called Rebekah Alice and Esther Joy! A fun note here is that my grandmother, your great-grandmother in the states, is also Alice."

1-12-01 "I mailed your backpacks today to Love Basket. They are going over at the end of January to see you. Sounds like Muthu, your caregiver, will be traveling with you to the United States."

During our communication with the adoption agency, we were given opportunity to be as involved in the process as possible. Part of that process was to prepare little backpacks for our daughters to have while on their long flight to Minnesota. We filled each one with coloring books, crayons, a journal, stickers, and a couple of smaller toys to help pass the time.

1-21-01 "We received clearance from the organization that will provide your passports. It looks like we will be meeting you in Minneapolis towards the middle or end of February. I have arranged to be off from work by March 1st until the end of the school year. All in His timing! We wait. We love you!"

2-14-01 "Happy Valentine's Day! God bless you! You're on your way soon. We await a phone call about your exact date of arrival. Love Basket just returned from visiting you once more. Your little ten year old friend that you played with each day in India, just left for Spain. They said you are having a tough time, Rebekah. We are preparing your room. I just couldn't sleep. It is about 4:30 a.m. and I've been reading some of Mother Teresa's book. Such truth.

Such peace. May I be able to step beyond as she did and simply live where He is calling. We await your blessed arrival!"

"Every good and perfect gift is from above, coming down from the Father of lights, with Whom there is no variation or shifting shadow."
James 1:17

The pages in my journal have run out. The final sticky note which still clings to the last page reads...

IMPORTANT MESSAGE

Flight 396

Arriving Thursday,

February 22, 2001

8:40 p.m. Minneapolis

The Airport

The drive to Minneapolis was a blur. Our older four stayed the night at Grandpa and Grandma's in order for Pete and I to focus on the needs of Rebekah and Esther. We arrived early enough to wait in the Minnesota winter darkness. As I traced my finger along the glass pane window in the airport, it felt cold. My thoughts lingered as I stared into the night, waiting for some sight of the plane on which they would arrive. Thoughts raced through my mind. What if they were delayed in customs? What if they missed their connection half way around the world? What if they won't be coming?

We rechecked the flight numbers that were to be arriving from Los Angeles. We frantically began looking on every monitor possible, and to our dismay…there existed absolutely NO flight #396 whatsoever! We had no phone numbers to make calls to our agency, and at this dark hour, they were indeed closed. More red flags began waving before me, and my panic buttons were beginning to sound their alarms. We did notice, however, that there was one flight coming in at the very time ours should to be arriving, but the numbers did not match. The monitor claimed it was Flight #306, but we had no way to confirm it.

We had little time to ponder our dilemma as minutes later, the announcement came that Flight #306 had indeed landed from Los Angeles. We could only wait and hope.

There were many people standing by to meet others who would soon be getting off the plane. I could not sit still. I moved from one place to another, pushing my way to the front of the crowd as people began to exit the plane. At this point, Pete simply took my arm and pulled me back from my incessant gawking and peering at every passenger exiting the flight.

"Relax," he said. "They'll be getting off soon...just relax!" Passenger after passenger disembarked from the aircraft. For minutes...people filed past us...but still, no little girls! Soon, it was I who was pulling on Pete's arm and calming him as he began pushing his way forward.

More thoughts ran through my mind. I'd heard about this kind of stuff on TV. People take your money, and you end up with no kids! I envisioned us standing in front of the cameras, telling the world our pathetic story.

At this point, the flow of passengers off that airplane, had come to a halt. We stood staring at the now vacant doorway, and the world seemed to stop. Our emotions matched the temperature outside as our hearts dropped in heaviness trying to understand what could have possibly happened to our little crew.

Then, out of nowhere, came the final three passengers from Flight #306!

Two little girls were jabbering like they had a story to tell, and the youngest one's hands were flailing as she spoke. There, before us, stood the two most beautiful little girls in the world! Even though we were indoors, their teeth chattered as they stood in their light weight summer dresses. Two familiar backpacks were spotted in the hand of their caregiver, Muthu. At that moment, those backpacks were the only possessions they had in the world.

Esther saw us and marched right over. She continued to speak her verbal lingo in her native language, Tamil. Rebekah followed. Standing back she softly observed what Esther was saying, and, with a gentle smile, nodded in agreement. Esther was holding a small family picture album we had sent in the first packet, months earlier. Pointing to our pictures, she clearly and confidently spoke, "Mommy? Daddy?"

I took my finger and traced the shape of a heart over my own. Moving the outlined shape over their hearts, I whispered the words to them for the very first time... "I love you!"

We made our way from the airport. Escorting Muthu to a van, he would soon be able to rest before his flight out the next day. Down into the parking ramp we went, gathering the girls into our vehicle for the journey home. However, we soon found ourselves sidetracked as Rebekah and Esther became intrigued with a few pieces of paper strewn upon the ground. These papers took the form of little golden parking ramp tickets, and each time they saw one, they grasped and grabbed as many as they could take hold of for our journey home.

We drove on into the night. I will forever remember the city lights shining down upon our little caravan as we made our way home. Within minutes, Esther nodded off. Rebekah's beautiful almond eyes followed each light, each movement... everything within her view. But even with the excitement of all that was new...she, too, could not stave off the sleep that eventually overcame her.

The Journey Home

The return trek was a five hour car ride home. We made one stop at a gas station for a bathroom break. This stop brought the dome light on in our vehicle, and as Rebekah's eyes opened, we heard her first English word spoken! "Appo!" She pointed frantically at an apple that was sitting near the front seat. As the agency had been working with their home in India, the workers had taught them a few basic English words. Besides the nursery rhymes we'd watched them perform on video, apparently Rebekah had also learned the word, "APPLE!"

By 3:00 a.m. we had arrived home, and in the door they burst. Grabbing blankets they found, along with benches and any other make shift items, they built themselves an area of safety in which to sit. "Child's play," is what we thought it was, but as the weeks went on, we knew that each time they would do this, it simply brought security into their world. Borders and boundaries in which they had some control would eventually be broken with love, trust, and routine within our family.

I would be remiss not to mention that before laying them down for the first night's sleep, we decided to do a little lice treatment as recommended by our agency. So…in the early morning hours, although we were sure they had already been treated before arriving, we decided to take this precaution before placing them in their beds that were ready and waiting.

As I began combing through their hair, we noticed that the problem looked to be just a little bigger than anticipated. We continued the treatment on into the early morning hours. Once the problem had been conquered, they were able to get the long awaited sleep in their beds.

Waking up the next morning and taking a fresh look at the situation we decided more help was needed. By late morning our family hair dresser, Sarah, had arrived to minister in our home. By the time she left, she had given beautiful buzz cuts that cleared up the problem, and also allowed us to move towards the much needed bonding process.

As I look back, the contribution Sarah made to our family was nothing less than a gift. She showed up with nothing but love. Her patience and understanding brought an acceptance that will forever be held in our hearts. She set the pace for our older children to enter our home, meet their siblings, and do so for the first time without the fear of catching those friendly buggers that had arrived without boarding passes or passports!

Just before leaving, our dear friend turned to us with clippers in hand and simply said, "Here...you can keep these!" With a smile on her face, she presented the clippers to us to do as we pleased. Needless to say, we formally discarded them into the garbage, never to look back on the problem again!

The Days and Weeks Ahead

The firsts were amazing to be a part of. The first time they met their siblings...the first horseback ride and Pete was the horse...the first time they saw their glittery white teddy bears purchased just for them...the first Easter baskets with all that candy...the first outing in the snow...the first time they saw the cat through the glass door, not realizing that there was actually separation between them...and the first of all firsts was their first bubble bath.

The giggles, the laughter, the jumping against the shower stall as if it were a slide... helping them to land in the lush white puddles of bubbles, was more fun than any theme park could have provided!

We stepped out with them into a world from which they could now launch. The days that followed were nothing short of miraculous. There were times of laughter; there were times of tears. There were tender moments of bonding, growing, and giving selflessly in order to knit two more lives into our family. We grew. All eight of us grew and are continuing to grow. There are lumps, and there are bumps, but the journey is one we would do over in a heartbeat!

May your heart, too, beat in some way for adoption.
And, the question still remains...
Is there room at the Inn?
Is there room for one...just one more?

I Love You Big!

"I LOVE YOU BIG"... is what I think as I watch the darkened airport sky, face pressed upon the glass window as I wait and watch for the arrival of two little girls to have and to hold. The big plane finally lands and we wait.

"I LOVE YOU BIG"... is what I say in my mind as many people file off the plane and we wait a long time. Finally, two little girls with big brown eyes quietly step off and smile.

"I LOVE YOU BIG" ... is what our faces tell one another as we stoop and give our hearts through our eyes, and our smiles. "Mommy? Daddy? You softly say.

"I LOVE YOU BIG" ... is what I feel as I trace a heart shape on my chest and transfer the outline to your shirts. With a smile and a hug, you grab hold of our hands, and we head for home.

"I LOVE YOU BIG" ... is what I try to prepare with my hands as we grapple for bananas, apples, eggs and your orders bark loudly for "peanut butter, NO! Jam, YES!"

"I LOVE YOU BIG" ... is what I whisper into your ears as you line your dollies all in a row for baths and sprinkles of "powda", bringing your worlds into order while modeling daily life you'd lived for the past several years in a land far away.

"I LOVE YOU BIG" … is what we show you through our laughter, while mingled with yours as the tickle sessions turn into horseback rides on Daddy's back.

"I LOVE YOU BIG" … are the words I say to my girls as you snuggle down into bed. With a smack of a kiss on the cheek, you cozy down with your pink blankies.

WELCOME HOME! I will always, ***"LOVE YOU BIG!"***

So often times we like to linger after reading a book. We long for just a little bit more before we close the covers. I hope you will enjoy reading a few more stories as much as I did remembering them. Blessings, and Thank You for being part of our family through the sharing of our lives.

♥

The Golden Ticket

Flutter, flutter, SWOOSH! As the little feet landed upon the cement stairwell, the chase was on. Golden tickets everywhere! The swirling was set in motion each time the parking ramp door opened. As the wind whistled the feather weight paper into action, the exhilarating chase began anew!

Two little pairs of hands, along with the feet, wistfully played the game of "Catch the Tickets!" Giggles and laughter spilled out as the "Level 3 Golden Ramp" tickets floated upward, catching a ride with each gust of cold air. When fists were filled and the laughter subsided, they counted their booty while making their getaway into the dark of the night.

Child's play was all it was. Now, the little golden tickets sit in a glass jar upon the shelf, and are worth more than all the precious metal in the world. These tickets were purchased with a price. The price was trust. The price was giving up homeland. The price was being too little to have a choice in their lives, or the circumstances surrounding the travel it took to grab the gold.

You see, it all began in a land far away and would span over three countries. It was a plan by design. The design was rooted in faith that by following a desire within hearts, there would be an end. What that end would look like, was not clear but the little golden tickets were like bread crumbs along the journey of trust.

It all began one day when visiting a children's home far away. We met two little people who needed a home. The process to adopt was birthed. The road took an unexpected turn and the children sent elsewhere. With tears and inner turmoil, another country was then chosen, and the wait was on.

One day, the phone call came. Soon, two little girls flew half way around the world only to land in a stairwell chasing golden tickets wherever the wind did blow. Chase them they did…with laughter…with delight…with trust…with love for life and with equal delight, they have become part of our home, and a part of us.

Oh, it wasn't all that easy but truth-be-told, it wasn't all that hard. There were hours of paper work, but little by little, inch by inch, it was a cinch. There were hours of waiting…and trusting…and praying. And, in the end…each one turned out to be a golden ticket!

"And I will fill this house with glory says the Lord of hosts…and in this place I will give peace…" Haggai 2:7-9. Amen.

Minneapolis-St. Paul
International Airport

**Gold
Ramp**

3 GOLD

**General
Parking
Level
3**

DUCKY DOOLITTLE

(A true story about Rebekah)

"Mom, I have to tell you something!" The statement was a rather open ended telephone conversation, causing my mind to wonder what exactly had happened. I prepared myself for a confession of sorts. After all, that's how they usually start. The voice was rather shaky, and I thought it was evidence enough that they were expecting a reprimand from my end. It took seconds to realize that this was not the case, and the shakiness in her voice turned to excitement as her story unfolded.

"I was shooting hoops when all of a sudden I heard a little peeping sound. I followed the sound, and, when I looked down, right by the tree next to the dog kennel was a little tiny baby duck! I have it in the house now, and we put him in a box and…" The story went on in detail as to how she was now taking care of this little baby duck that apparently had no next of kin.

Once arriving home, I saw that she was right; it was tiny. The little fluffy thing must have been no bigger than three inches high and even less than that wide. Fluffy, fat, and feisty, Ducky Doolittle was here to stay. At least that's what we were all hoping for. You see, we've had creatures from the wild before, and they just never seemed to survive. We were all hoping that this time things would be different.

I made my way over to the box and noticed that the little thing already had a wonderful cushion of long green handpicked grass, a Tupperware pond placed centerfield, and a Beanie Baby for bonding purposes. As the evening wore on, I found him curled upon the lap of another, and wrapped in the fluffiest winter scarf to be had. Never mind that he chose to do a little *business* here and there. We were, after all, officially adopting the little thing and it just came with the territorial duties. For once, the cleanup crews didn't seem to mind all that much and rose to the occasion without being asked. Ducky seemed to like us, and we all knew we loved him.

However, sometimes love just isn't enough. You see, he had free will and a few untamed characteristics that made him squirt right out of our hands every so often. One minute we'd be holding him, and the next, well…he'd be on the hard wood floor without much warning at all. Quickly bouncing back into form, we didn't think much of it. We didn't think much of it that is, until he curled up into his little corner and just didn't move any more. That was the end of Ducky Doolittle.

Hearts melted for him, and tears were shed. As I made my way out onto the front porch, the empty box now stood as evidence of the memories he'd given us. Straightening the coat rack I saw the winter scarf he'd once cuddled with...and there, in the laundry room, was his favorite Beanie Baby. Hours later, while transferring the washed items into the dryer, out fluttered a long blade of grass that once had been picked just for him. Whether or not Ducky was with us, he touched our lives, and he had allowed us to love him even if he was unaware of the fact that he did so.

 Dear Lord, many times there are those around us who touch our lives: a helping hand, a pat on the back, a smile, a word of encouragement, a card, a letter, a blade of grass cut. Those are the recognizable moments; a few simple accepted gestures of love. Then, there are other times when free will enters in and simple gestures of love are rejected. The love poured out ends up in a corner somewhere...appearing to be, for a while, a little pile of deathlike stillness on the party it was poured out upon. However, Your word says, "Love never ends." In that we find faith and when the seeds of love appear to be dormant, we know that they were planted and someday flowers will bloom. For in the end, truly, we are called to love and the fruit of that love is Yours...for Your glory. Amen.

♥

MIRACLE ON 440TH STREET

(A true story about Esther)

The time? 11:30 p.m. stateside.
The time? 11:30 a.m. Chennai, India.

Blankly, I stared at the $58 bill I'd just received for my computer anti-virus protection. As I glanced over at my computer screen, the flashing red X across the symbol of my provider reminded me that the virus protection had not been working for the past several months. Now, I was supposed to pay for yet another download that wouldn't download!

I began dialing the 800 number on the statement and was going to cancel it altogether, when a young man answered. The accent was all too familiar, and as he spoke, it reminded me of only one word. *BUCHUKARA!*

Eight years earlier, that familiar accented word rolled off the tongue of our youngest, adopted from Chennai, India. Although we could make out the word, the meaning of it was much less clear.

Over and over again, the word *BUCHUKARA* was heard. Judging by the desperate tones of when it was used, and in the various situations it was thrown at us, the closest thing we could come up with was "Boogie Man!" As the years slipped by, we heard it less frequently until altogether, it stopped.

As life would have it, we met various people from their homeland and inevitably, our conversation would find its way to this mysterious word...*BUCHUKARA*. And, time after time, it remained a mystery. Facial expressions drew puzzled looks as nobody seemed to know what it meant, and worse yet, declared it to be sheer nonsense. However, in my heart of hearts...I knew...I just knew...there was more to it.

Tonight, my mind tried hard to focus as to why I had called this person to whom I was speaking, and as I listened to his sales pitch, I just had to ask.

"Where are you? I mean...which country are you working in?"

The friendly young voice responded to my question, but I already knew the answer. "Chennai, India," he said.

Bypassing my reason for calling, I got right to the point. "So, what does the word, *Buchukara* mean?" I rolled it off my tongue quickly, hoping he might hear something familiar.

"That is not a word in my language, ma'am," he said.

"Oh," I said explaining my plight as to why I wanted to know more about it. Moving into the real reason for calling, the word slipped out one more time, and although miles away, I could sense him coming to attention.

"Ahhh...." he softly stated, "I know what that word means…"

Time froze. My heart stopped. I did not want to miss a single word of what he was about to tell me. I listened intently as he simply said, "That word means…HOLD ME!"

And, in that split-second of time…it all made sense.

I went on to tell him that it was snowing in Minnesota, and he informed me that it was raining in Chennai. I shared that it was 11:30 p.m. stateside, and he reported it to be twelve hours difference from his vantage point on the globe.

Step by step, he went on to not only fix my computer problem but to ultimately gift us with a miracle, here on 440th Street.

Dear Lord, 'tis the season when it was nothing short of a miracle that love came down on Christmas Day. In Psalm 38:15 it says, "I wait for you, O Lord; you will answer, O'Lord my God." And…you did answer. And, you continue to answer. Amen.

God bless your very own heart journey!

Rebekah Alice Kjolhaug

My name is Rebekah. I just want to say that adoption is the happiest feeling in a person's life. Seeing that you have a mom and a dad, fills so many empty holes in your heart. I know that every single person in the world wants to be touched with care, read to at bedtime, hugged with love, and have a special person in their life that they know will be there for them in happiness or sorrow.

I have lots of family members who are so dear to me. My brothers and sisters are wonderful. They have helped me to grow and make good choices in my life. They are always there for me.

I was seven years old when I came to America. Now I am sixteen, and my life is so wonderful. I have lots of new friends and many hobbies. My favorite sport is basketball. I love to draw and read. When I graduate, I want to be a baby doctor. I love caring for young ones and seeing them smile.

Someday, I want to go back to India and see the orphanage where I lived. Maybe, just maybe I will be able to find my grandma who brought me to the orphanage after my mom died. I pray for her and any other family I might still have.

I would definitely recommend adoption because you are giving that child a future to live and to shine. You are giving that child happiness and especially, you are giving that child love.

Love,

Rebekah Alice

Rebekah Alice

Esther Joy Kjolhaug

My name is Esther Joy Kjolhaug. I am fourteen years old and came here when I was five. I'm in eighth grade now and love my friends at school and especially my friends at youth group. My middle name is Joy because my birth mom's name was Joy.

She was a Christian, and she loved me very much. I am glad she was a Christian because I know I will see her again. I miss her. Sometimes when I look in the sky at night, I can see only one star. I like to pretend it is my mom looking down and watching everything I do. If I had only one wish, I wish I could have a picture of what she looked like. I don't remember what she looks like. Sometimes when I get good grades or do good at a basketball game, I think my birth mom would be proud of me.

It's hard to explain to people how my life was before I came here. They ask questions and try to understand. Most of the time people ask questions because they are curious, but sometimes they say silly things. One time a lady at a restaurant asked my mom if she bought me on the internet. We laughed really hard because we knew she really didn't know what she was talking about.

Adoption to me is like the biggest wish anyone could ever hope for. I think that when one child finds out that a family wants them, their life lights up. I think that is so amazing when one person can change another person's life like that. If you ever think about adopting a child, the other amazing thing is that it will change your life too.

I am so glad to be where I am. I am also glad that I now have so many people that love me and care about me. They look after me. I hope one day you can experience the chance to light up someone's life. You will make them smile just because little kids want someone to love them. They don't care if you are not perfect or your house isn't perfect or if there are struggles. They just are glad to have your love and care.

I thank God each and every day for the love in this new family that He gave me.

Love,

Esther Joy

Esther Joy

Suggested Steps to Follow on Your Journey

The steps to adopt often times may appear to be overwhelming. However, the basics are very simple. The following will provide an outline of how to begin…

- ♥ Pray about adopting. It is important to know that initially, it is not unusual for one spouse to be hesitant, but it is important that ultimately both individuals agree on adopting. There are recommended reads listed in the back of this book that may help answer your questions.

- ♥ Choose an adoption agency that is a good match for you. Do they handle both domestic and international adoptions? If so, which countries do they represent? Talk to others who have utilized their services.

- ♥ Call the agency and ask that they send you their informational packets. Visit their websites. There is no charge for asking questions. Again, a few adoption resources are listed in the back of this book.

- ♥ Did I mention that you should choose an agency? There are enough emotional ups and downs in this process. The enjoyment comes in keeping your eyes on the goal. Let the agency handle the "red tape." Most are non-profit. The fees that are charged for the adoption process are needed to pay for flights, care-givers, and court systems. Find a reputable agency, and let them do the work.

- Follow the steps they provide for you. They will keep you updated as the process progresses. If you have questions, don't hesitate to contact your agency. It is important that you understand the process and the paperwork you are doing.

- Finances may be of concern. There are tax credits and loans specifically for adoption. Trust that God will meet you where you are at, know that He is able and find comfort in Him being in control.

- Enjoy the process. You are adding to your family and making "room for one more at the Inn."

- Sometimes we think that if we don't do it, someone else will. Truth-be-told, sometimes if we don't do it, no one else does.

Acknowledgements

Blessings to the following people who helped breathe life into the words you just read.

Joni Woelfel, author and dear friend, who always believes the best in me. (www.aplaceoflight.com)

Pete, my husband, who is truly the rock within our home.

Luke, Maria, Heidi, Christopher, Rebekah, and Esther, our children, who laughed and cried as we remembered the episodes presented in this book.

Tim, Dena, Josh, Ben, and Maria Stromstad, founders of Homes of Life in Costa Rica and Guatemala, for connecting so many dots in our lives and nudging the dream by living it out. (www.homesoflife.org)

Candace Pauley, who gave tremendous insight into the process of adoption and held our hearts along the way.

Frank Block (Executive Director of Love Basket), **Kate Powers, Geetha and Muthu**, who loved and cared for our children years before we ever laid eyes on them.

Love Basket an agency with a heart for children around the world. (www.lovebasket.org)

Roxanne Stordahl, who dreams dreams while whispering into hearts what she sees and hears.

Katie Krogstad, who puts wings to dreams and tells you they are possible! (www.sugarbrookecreative.com)

Last but not least, **Karen and Norm Knudsen**, founders of Mercy Smiles International who lit the initial spark. Without their hearts given to children around the world…there would have been no path on which to travel. (www.mercysmiles.org)

"May all who come behind us find us faithful."
Steve Green

To order additional copies of
LOVE YOU BIG: *The Heart Journey of Adoption*
or The Heart *Journal* of Adoption, please visit:
www.sugarbrookecreative.com or call (701) 361-1368

Additional Resources
"Love Basket Adoption Agency"
(The agency mentioned in this book)
www.lovebasket.org

"God's Children Adoption Agency Inc."
1-877-233-2025
www.adoptgodschildren.com

"Homes of Life" Atenas, Costa Rica
Provides sponsorship and homes
for abandoned & abused children.
www.homesoflife.org

"Focus on the Family"
Colorado Springs, Colorado
*Exceptional resources not only for
adoption, but for the whole family.*
1-800-A-FAMILY
www.focusonthefamily.org

Recommended Reads
"*125 Most Asked Questions About Adoption*" by Paul Baldwin
"*The Adoption Decision*" by Laura Christianson
"*While We Wait*" by Heidi Schumpf

About the Author

Kathleen is a wife, mother, teacher, and writer. Her weekly newspaper column, *Theology in the Trenches,* is published throughout Minnesota and Montana. As a former Peace Corps Volunteer and a short term missionary, Kathleen enjoys traveling beyond the borders of the family homestead in Northern Minnesota. However, most precious to her is her Lord and Savior...who so graciously forgives her of all her shortcomings. She is who she is only by the grace of God. Amen